Epic Fish Adult Coloring Book

BY SUSAN POTTERFIELDS

ISBN: 10: 1535100354
ISBN-13: 978-1535100359

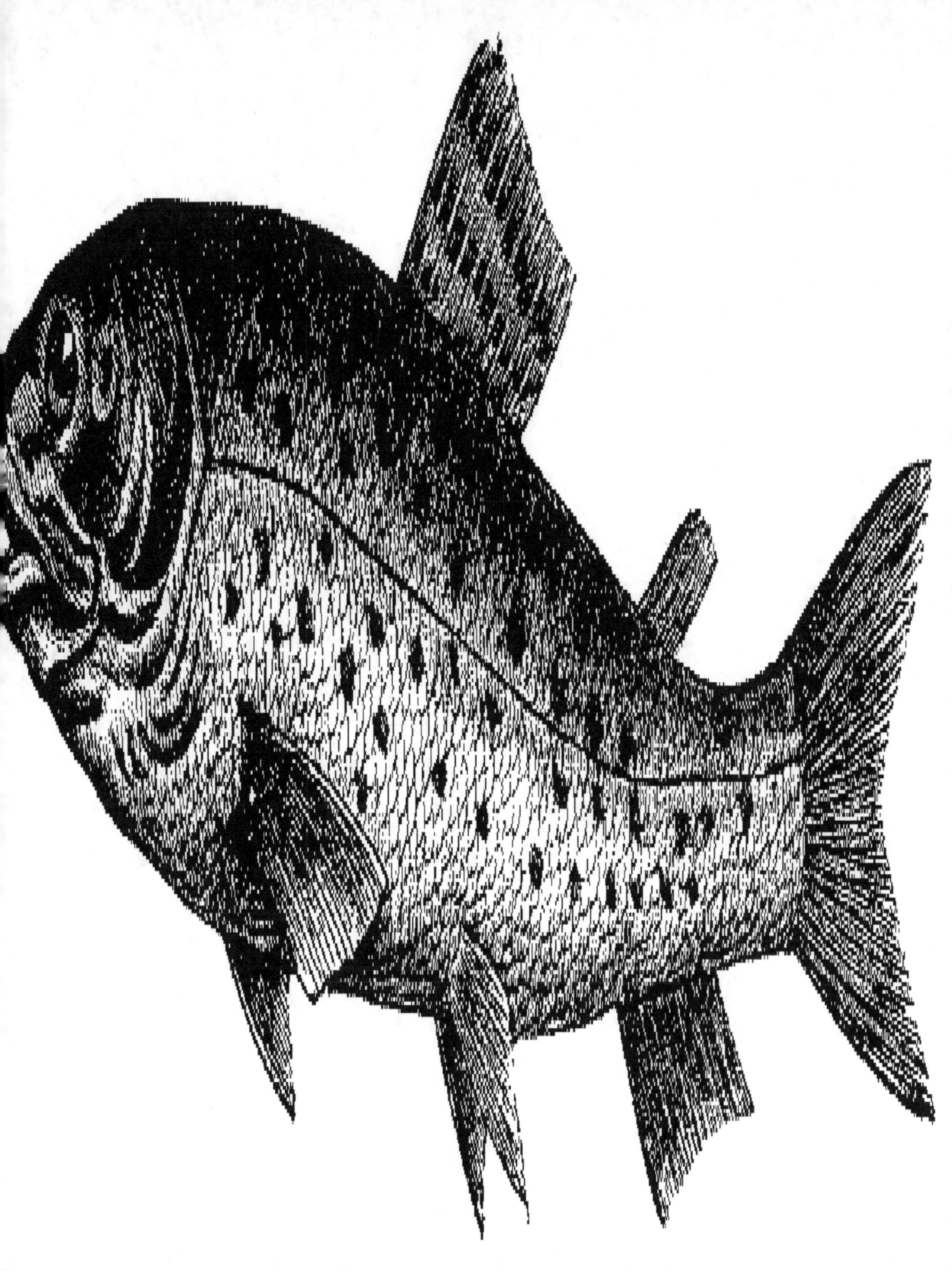

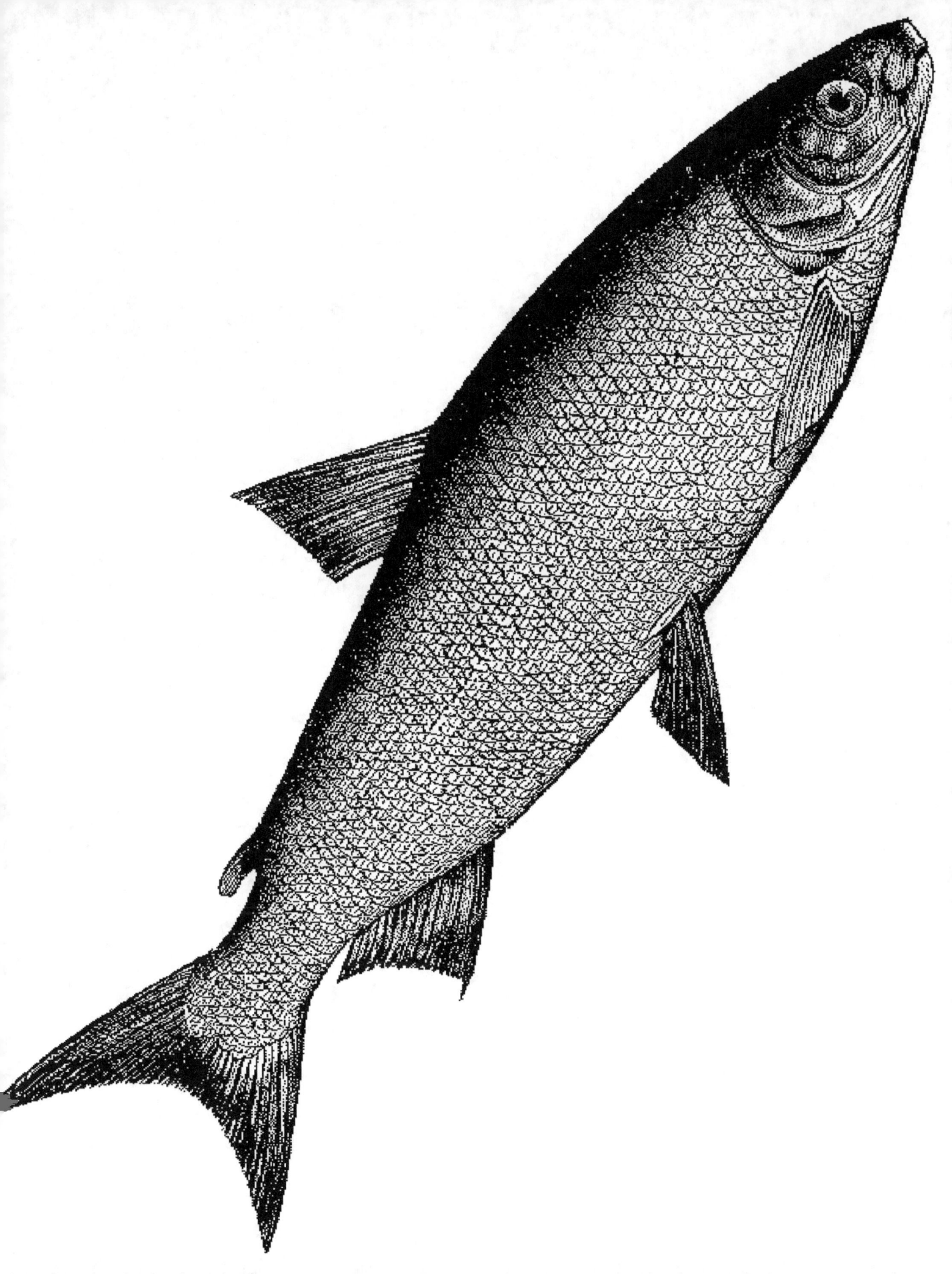

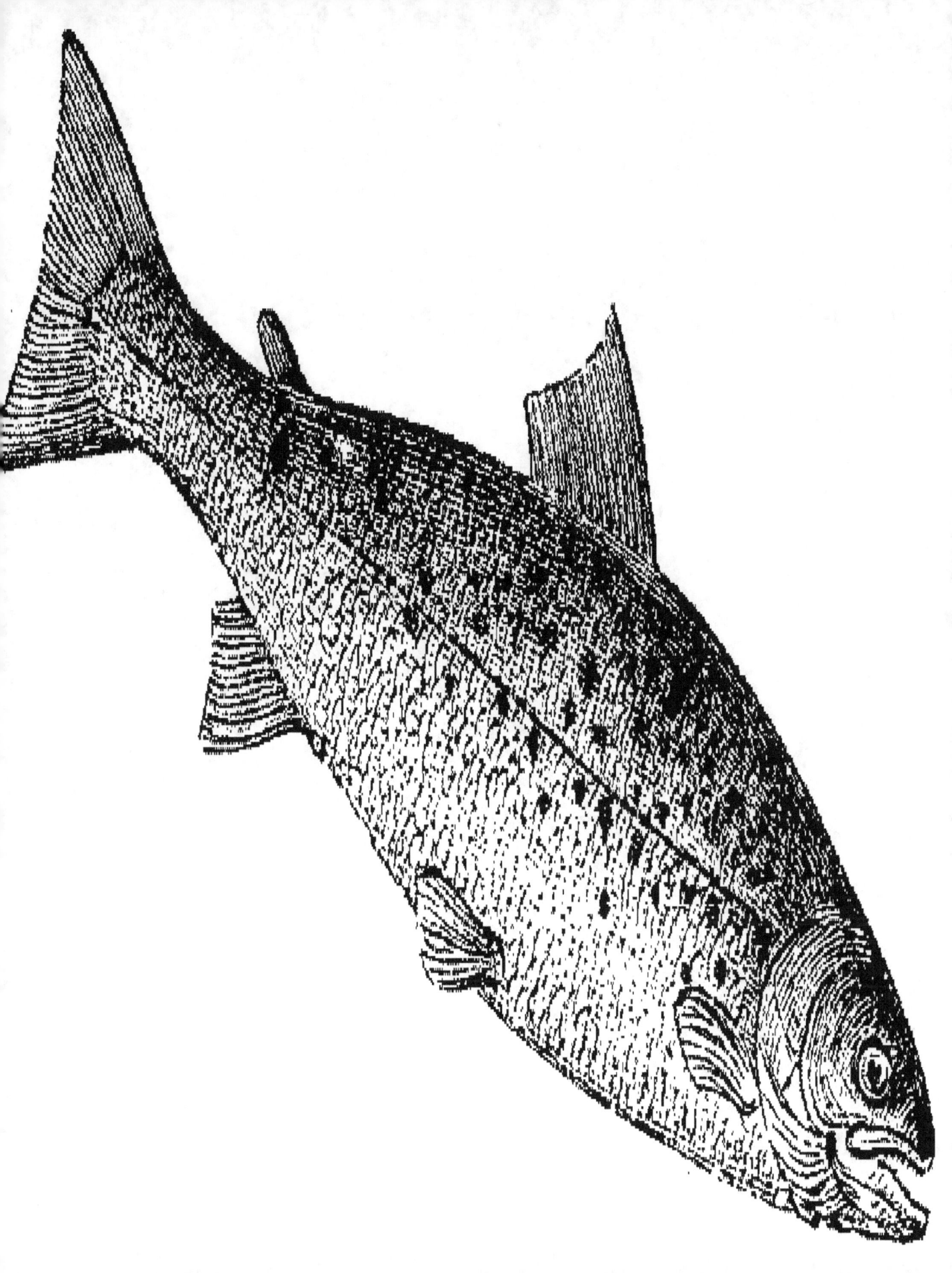

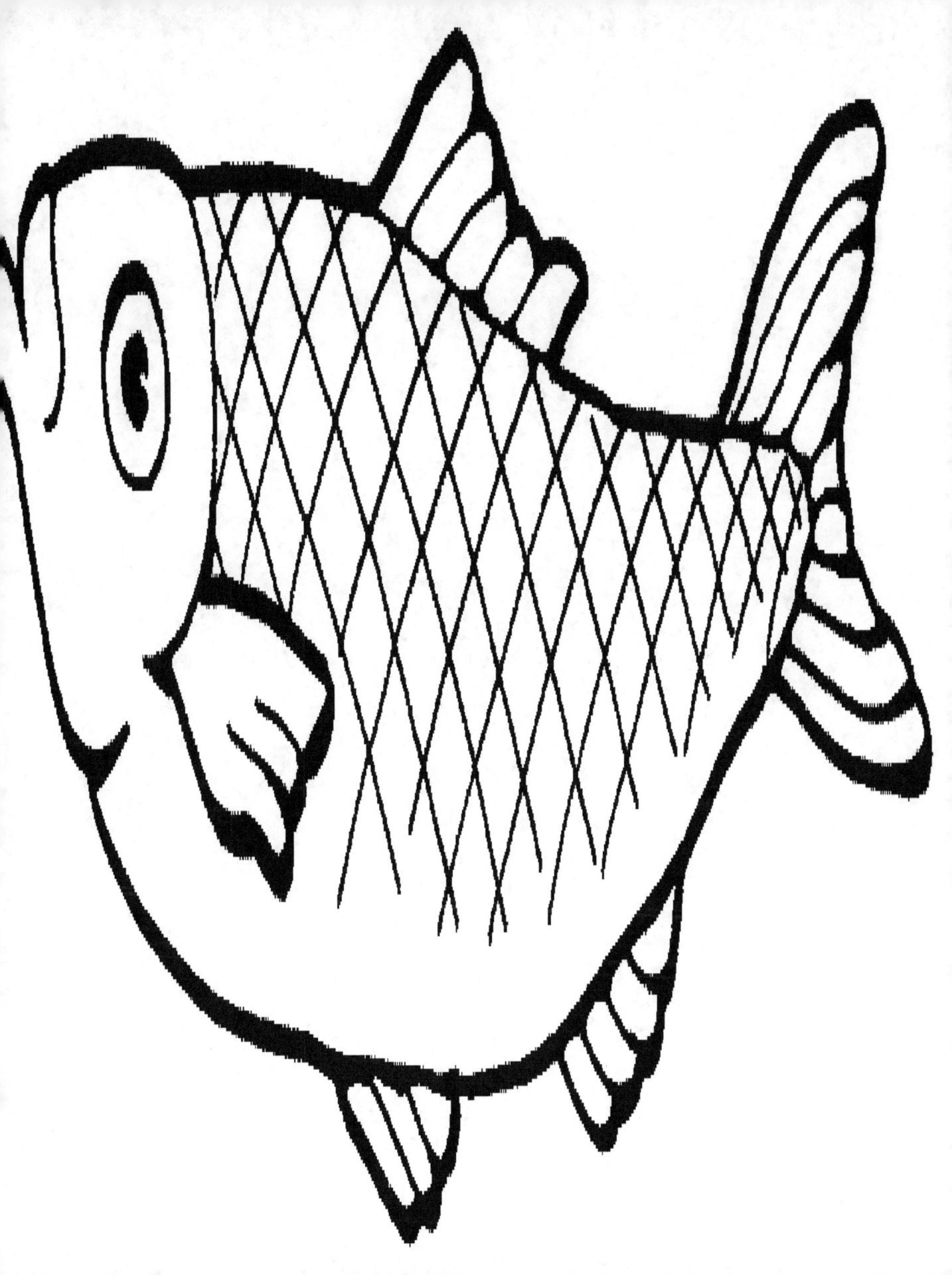

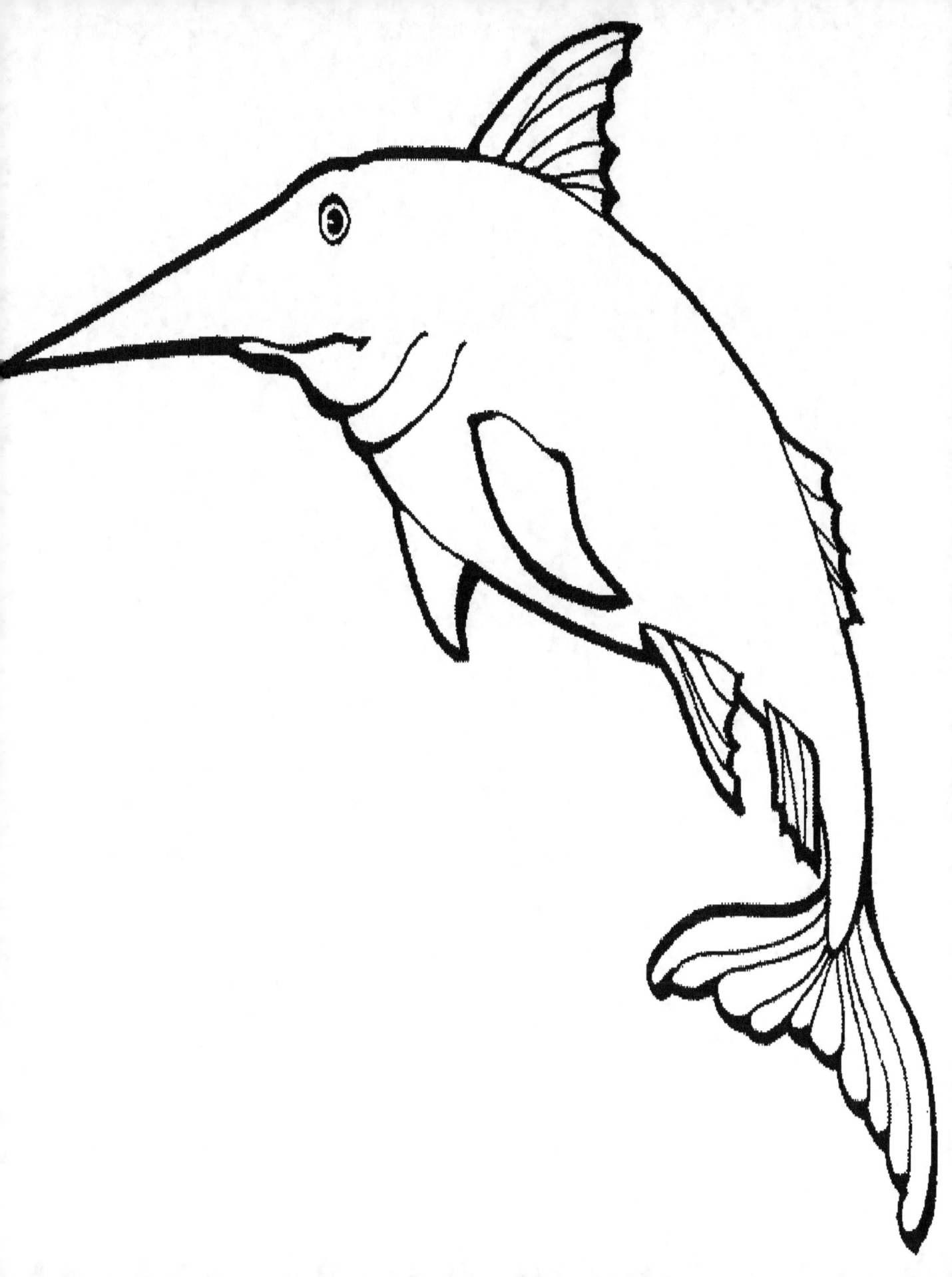

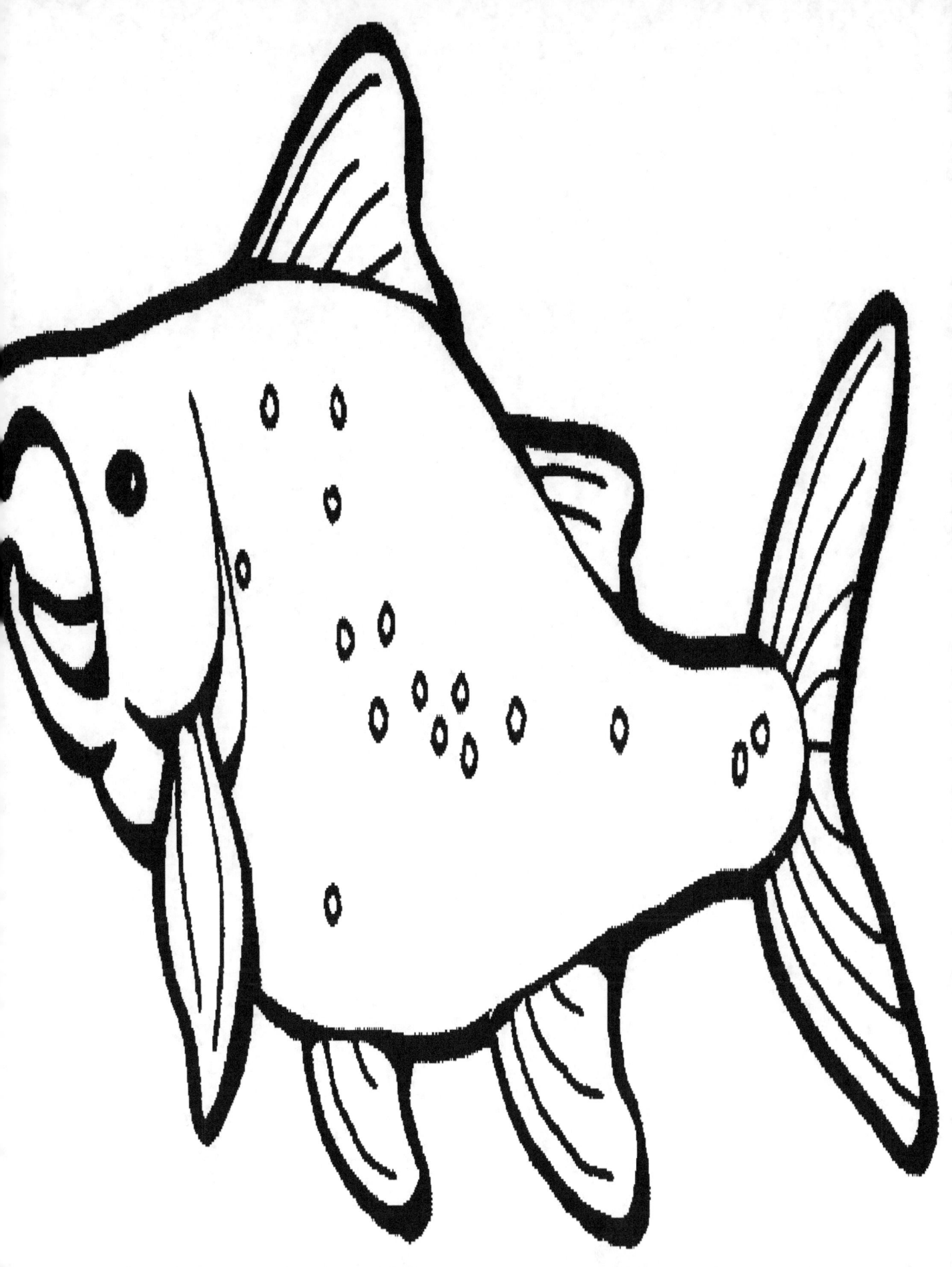

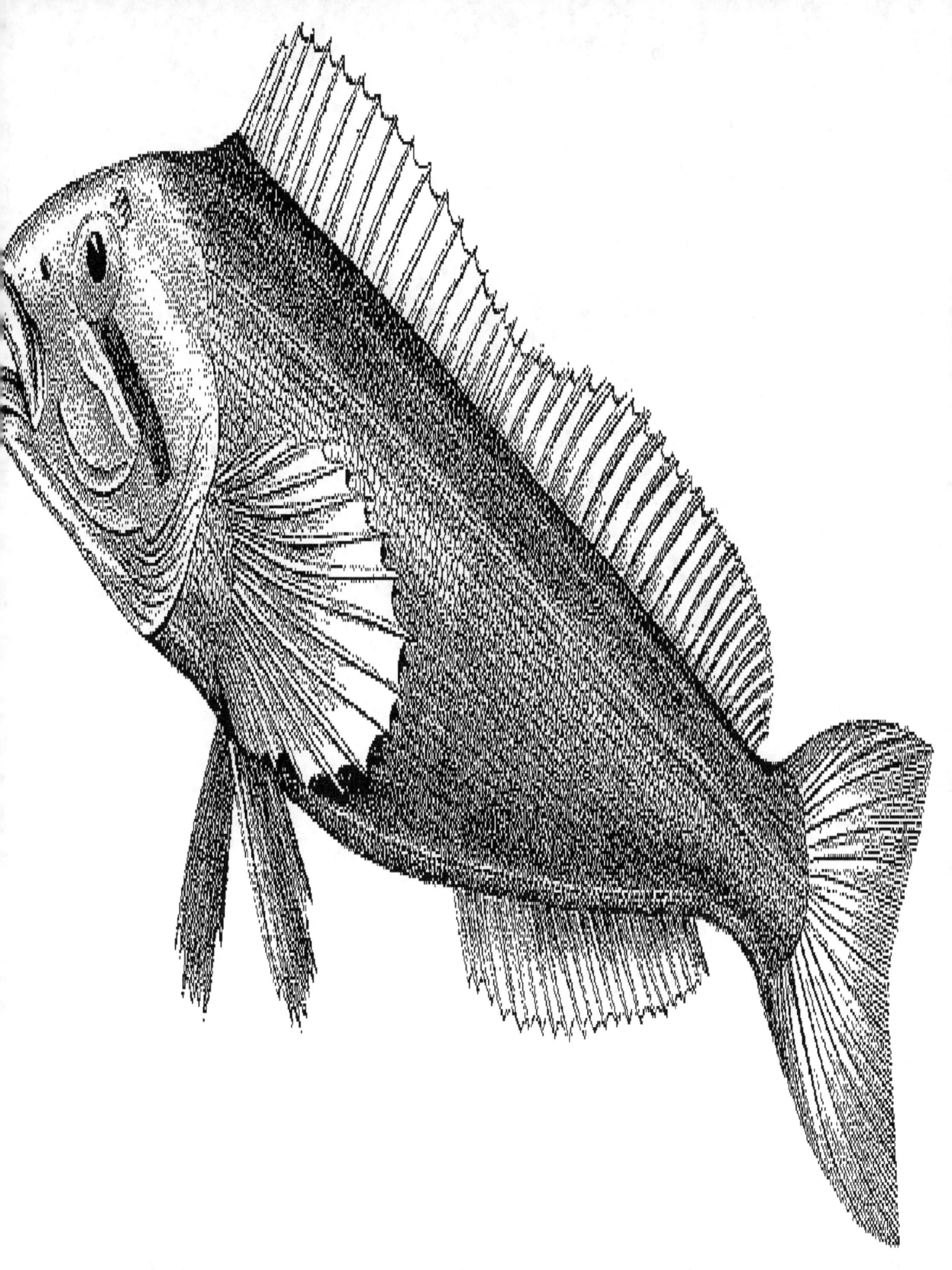

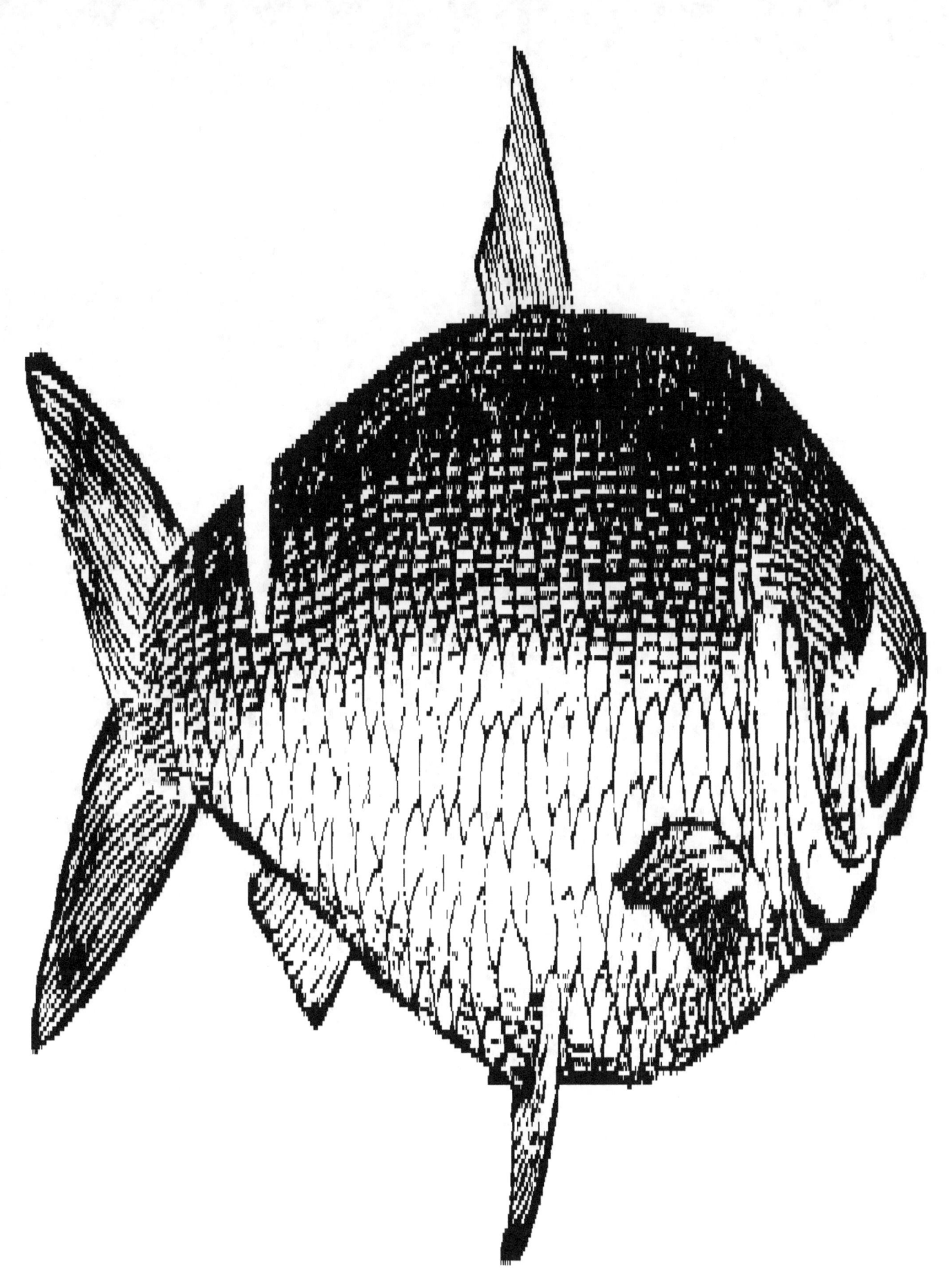

Other Coloring Books By Susan Potterfields

Epic Cat Adult Coloring Book
Epic Dog Adult Coloring Book
Epic Cow Adult Coloring Book
Epic Chicken Adult Coloring Book
Epic Dolphin Adult Coloring Book
Epic Crab Adult Coloring Book
Epic Bear Adult Coloring Book
Epic Turkey Adult Coloring Book
Epic Boar Adult Coloring Book
Epic Sheep Adult Coloring Book
Epic Rabbit Adult Coloring Book
Epic Pig Adult Coloring Book

And Many More

www.ingramcontent.com/pod-product-compliance
Lightning Source LLC
Chambersburg PA
CBHW082014290526
45787CB00016B/2934